Hot and

Written by Jo Windsor

PEARSON

Some animals live
in very hot places.
These animals know
how to keep cool.

Some animals live
in very cold places.
These animals know
how to keep warm.

This rabbit lives
in a very hot place.
It can go into the shade
to keep cool.

This snake lives
in a very hot place.
It can go under the rock
to keep cool.

This rat lives
in a very hot place.
It can go under the ground
to keep cool.

This fox lives
in a very hot place.
It can go under the ground
to keep cool, too.

This polar bear and her cubs
live in a very cold place.
They can go into a den
to keep warm.

This wombat lives
in a very cold place.
It can go under the ground
to keep warm, too.

The penguins live
in a very cold place.
The little penguins stand
on the big penguins' feet
to keep warm.

These monkeys live
in a very cold place.
They can go in the hot pools
to keep warm!

People who live in cold places
can keep warm, too.
They can wear warm clothes.

People who live in hot places
can keep cool, too.
They can wear cool clothes.

People know how to keep warm.
And people know
how to keep cool.

Index

Guide Notes

Title: Hot and Cold
Stage: Early (3) – Blue

Genre: Non-fiction
Approach: Guided Reading
Processes: Thinking Critically, Exploring Language, Processing Information
Visual Focus: Photographs (static images), Index
Word Count: 217

THINKING CRITICALLY
(sample questions)
- What do you think this book is going to tell us?
- What animals can you see on the front cover? Where do you think they live?
- Focus the children's attention on the index. Ask: "What animals are you going to find out about in this book?"
- If you want to find out about penguins, what page would you look on?
- If you want to find out about monkeys, what page would you look on?
- Look at pages 4 and 5. What do these animals do to keep cool?
- Look at pages 8 and 9. What do these animals do to keep warm?
- Look at page 10. How do you think the baby penguin will keep warm?
- If you are cold, what are some things you can do to get warm?

EXPLORING LANGUAGE

Terminology
Title, cover, photographs, author, photographers

Vocabulary
Interest words: shade, den, wombat
High-frequency words: how, very, these, who
Positional words: in, into, under, on
Opposites: hot – cold, warm – cool

Print Conventions
Capital letter for sentence beginnings, full stops, exclamation mark, commas